rib-ticklers
SPELLING
Strengthening Basic Skills with Jokes, Comics, and Riddles
GRADE 3

by Karen Latchana Kenney

Carson-Dellosa Publishing Company, Inc.

Greensboro, North Carolina

D1613620

Credits

Content Editor: Elizabeth Swenson

Copy Editors: Denise McAllister and Barrie Hoople

Layout and Cover Design: Nick Greenwood

Inside Illustrations: Robbie Short, Nick Greenwood, Chris Sabatino, and Christian Elden

Cover Illustration: Nick Greenwood

Table of Contents

Page Number	Commonly Misspelled Words & Homophones	Compound Words	Contractions	Digraphs & Silent Consonants	Double Consonants & Consonant Clusters	Prefixes, Suffixes, & Root Words	Syllables	Vowels	Word Endings & Plurals
5								●	
6								●	
7								●	
8								●	
9								●	
10								●	
11								●	
12								●	
13								●	
14								●	
15							●		
16							●		
17							●		
18							●		
19					●		●		
20							●		
21		●							
22		●							
23		●							
24					●				
25					●				
26					●				
27				●					
28				●					
29				●					
30				●	●				
31				●	●				
32				●	●				
33						●			
34						●			
35						●			
36						●			
37						●			
38						●			
39						●			

Page Number	Commonly Misspelled Words & Homophones	Compound Words	Contractions	Digraphs & Silent Consonants	Double Consonants & Consonant Clusters	Prefixes, Suffixes, & Root Words	Syllables	Vowels	Word Endings & Plurals
40						●			
41						●			
42						●			
43						●			
44						●			
45						●			
46						●			
47						●			
48									●
49									●
50									●
51									●
52									●
53									●
54									●
55	●								
56	●								
57				●					
58				●					
59				●					
60				●					
61	●								
62	●								
63	●								
64	●								
65	●								
66			●						
67			●						
68			●						
69			●						
70			●						
71			●						
72			●						
73			●						
74			●						

Bowling Cats

Write the word for each clue. To solve the riddle, write the boxed letters in order on the lines below.

> bait   bang   cane   catch   pale   same   tale   task   yam

1. a sudden and loud noise ___ ___ ___ ___

2. having very little color ___ ___ ___ ___

3. a story ___ ___ ___ ___

4. an object used to help someone walk ___ ___ ___ ___

5. a vegetable ___ ___ ___

6. the opposite of *throw* ___ ___ ___ ___ ___

7. not different ___ ___ ___ ___

8. what is used to catch a fish ___ ___ ___ ___

9. work that has been given to someone to do ___ ___ ___ ___

Answer: ___ ___ ___ ___ ___ ___ ___ ___ ___

   **5**

Name _____

Peanuts in Space

Circle each short *e* word. Then, write each short *e* word around the planet. The last letter of each word is the first letter of the next word. One has been done for you.

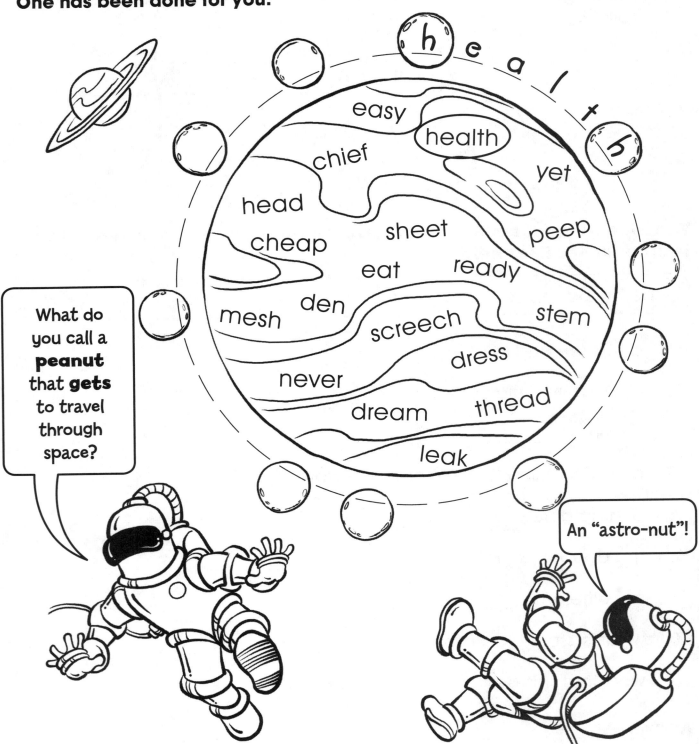

h e a l t h

easy
chief
health
yet
head
sheet
peep
cheap
eat
ready
den
stem
mesh
screech
dress
never
dream
thread
leak

What do you call a **peanut** that **gets** to travel through space?

An "astro-nut"!

Lions in the Garden

Circle each correctly spelled word and the letter beside it. To solve the riddle, write the circled letters in order on the lines below.

1. sick **a**   sieck **e**
2. wick **d**   wyck **y**
3. hike **a**   hyke **i**
4. sygh **c**   sigh **n**
5. sliep **t**   slip **d**
6. fiber **e**   fyber **m**
7. tietle **b**   title **l**
8. dyce **a**   dice **i**
9. stiele **f**   style **o**
10. wire **n**   wyre **s**

What **kind** of **lion** grows in a garden?

Answer: ____ _____ __ _ _____

Hot Duck

What do you call a **hot**, loud duck?

FIRE DEPT.

Unscramble each word. To solve the riddle, write the circled letters in order on the lines below.

1. totsa
   — — ⃝ — — —

2. xfo
   ⃝ — —

3. ongig
   — — ⃝ — —

4. preo
   — ⃝ — —

5. nbeo
   — — — ⃝ —

6. uoteq
   ⃝ ⃝ — — —

7. flao
   — — ⃝ —

8. hopc
   ⃝ — — —

9. klco
   — — ⃝ —

10. kjeo
    — — — ⃝

11. rcko
    ⃝ — — —

Answer:

___ " ___ ___ ___ ___ — ___ ___ ___ ___ "

Underwater Dance

How did **Hewy** the clam get hurt at the **underwater** dance?

He **pulled** a "mussel"!

Color the long *u* words yellow. Color the short *u* words red.

cube	much	mute	fuzz	cute
huge	tusk	fuel	puff	use
rescue	rush	few	plus	unit
bugle	drum	music	buzz	value
menu	dunk	pupil	bump	usual
argue	hush	view	dusk	beauty
review	hut	lump	nut	human

Late Broom

Circle each correctly spelled word and the letter beside it. To solve the riddle, write the circled letters in order on the lines below.

Why was the broom late?

1. eight   **I**
    aight   **L**
    ayaht   **A**

2. peeple   **b**
    people   **t**
    pieple   **l**

3. straight   **o**
    streyght   **t**
    streight   **r**

4. steyk   **u**
    staik   **e**
    steak   **v**

5. recieve   **m**
    receve   **p**
    receive   **e**

6. haight   **t**
    height   **r**
    heyght   **w**

7. island   **s**
    iland   **d**
    eiland   **y**

8. though   **w**
    thowgh   **r**
    thogh   **i**

9. beuty   **s**
    beauty   **e**
    bewty   **k**

10. sewe   **j**
    souw   **i**
    sew   **p**

11. buy   **t**
    bei   **h**
    bie   **f**

Answer:

____ ____   " ____ ____ ____ ____ – ____ ____ ____ ____ ____ ____ "!

Karate Class

Circle the 11 words in the puzzle. Then, write the words on the lines. Circle each letter that makes a short vowel sound.

d	o	e	s	k	o	u	g
p	l	a	i	d	z	a	o
e	f	p	l	a	u	g	h
b	r	h	w	g	k	g	b
e	i	a	s	p	g	g	u
e	e	l	a	r	u	i	i
n	n	f	i	i	e	v	l
t	d	m	d	e	s	e	d
w	x	m	t	n	s	y	w
b	u	s	y	r	j	y	y
o	w	d	y	b	b	l	r

_____

_____

_____

_____

_____

_____

_____

_____

_____

_____

_____

A Grizzly's Foot

Write the words in the correct columns.

bloom	boom	cook	good	hood	mood
stood	stool	tool	wood	woof	zoom

short *oo*, as in *book*　　　　　　　**long *oo*, as in *moon***

_____　　_____

_____　　_____

_____　　_____

_____　　_____

_____　　_____

Name _____

Corn on the Farm

Circle each correctly spelled word and the letter beside it. To solve the riddle, write the circled letters in order on the lines below.

Why was the **corn** mad at the **farmer**?

1. fern   **o**   furn   **n**

2. birn   **b**   burn   **n**

3. tirn   **j**   turn   **i**

4. virb   **v**   verb   **t**

5. burd   **j**   bird   **s**

6. dirt   **e**   durt   **o**

7. chirp   **a**   churp   **e**

8. nerse   **c**   nurse   **r**

9. germ   **s**   girm   **t**

Answer:

He pulled ____ ____   ____ ____ ____ ____   ____ ____ ____ ____ ____ !

Barber Race

Why did the **barber** win the race?

He knew a **shortcut!**

Draw a line through each word to complete the maze. Letters can connect down, left, and right. The first word has been done for you.

- ~~chair~~
- wear
- care
- share
- pear
- hair
- square

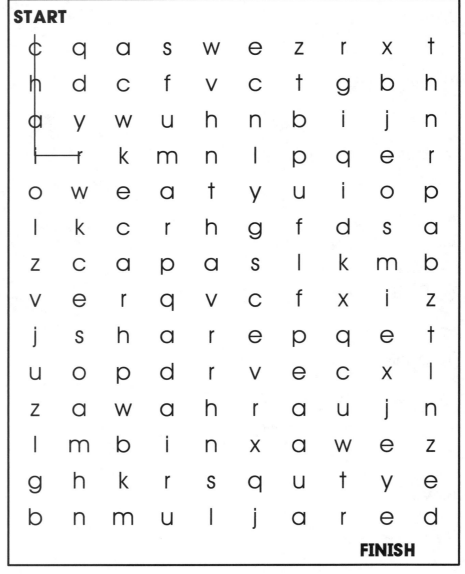

START

```
c q a s w e z r x t
h d c f v c t g b h
a y w u h n b i j n
r k m n l p q e r
o w e a t y u i o p
l k c r h g f d s a
z c a p a s l k m b
v e r q v c f x i z
j s h a r e p q e t
u o p d r v e c x l
z a w a h r a u j n
l m b i n x a w e z
g h k r s q u t y e
b n m u l j a r e d
```

FINISH

Name _____

Syllable Tug

Write the number of letters in each syllable. Circle the letter beside the larger number. Then, add the numbers in each column. To solve the riddle, write the circled letters in order on the lines below.

	Word	Syllables	First syllable	Second syllable
1.	quickly	quick/ly	5 (N)	2 M
2.	comfort		a	e
3.	plastic		i	l
4.	surface		s	t
5.	display		o	h
6.	witness		f	e
7.	problem		r	s
8.	vulture		u	s
9.	kingdom		i	e
10.	thunder		d	b
11.	jacket		e	n
12.	lobster		c	w
13.	program		j	i
14.	capture		p	n
15.	forward		g	s
16.	trumpet		I	Y
17.	chapter		t	k
18.	tortoise		h	s
19.	blanket		a	a
20.	crystal		t	l
21.	fancy		i	b
22.	construct		d	e

Total Letters: _____ _____

Which side wins the tug-of-war?

N ___ ___ ___ ___ ___   ___ ___ ___ ___ ___

___ ___ ___ ___ .   ___ ___ ___ '   ___ ___ ___ ___ ___ .

Long Distance Runners

Circle the letter beside each word that is correctly divided into syllables. Write the remaining words and divide them into syllables. To solve the riddle, write the circled letters in order on the lines below.

1. mu/sic **a** _____
2. red/uce **w** _____
3. re/cess **r** _____
4. fin/al **e** _____
5. hot/el **a** _____
6. ti/ger **i** _____
7. sil/ent **h** _____
8. lab/el **o** _____
9. fro/zen **v** _____
10. bab/y **b** _____
11. rob/ot **m** _____
12. va/por **e** _____
13. mom/ent **c** _____
14. ta/ken **r** _____

Answer:

____ ____ ____ ____ ____ ____

Piece of Cake

Why did the student eat his homework?

His teacher said that it was a piece of cake!

Circle the vowel pair or pairs in each word. Then, write each syllable on a separate line. Do not divide the vowel pairs.

1. creature _____ _____
2. caution _____ _____
3. author _____ _____
4. explain _____ _____
5. journey _____ _____
6. feature _____ _____
7. sweater _____ _____
8. moisture _____ _____
9. payment _____ _____
10. fountain _____ _____
11. receive _____ _____
12. weasel _____ _____
13. trouble _____ _____
14. mountain _____ _____
15. meadow _____ _____

Name _____

Puz/zle

Write the word for each clue and divide it into syllables. Then, complete the crossword puzzle.

> angle   little   middle   stable   staple   turtle   twinkle   uncle

Across

3. the way stars shine
_____ / _____

4. an animal that has a shell
_____ / _____

6. a piece of metal that holds papers together
_____ / _____

8. the corner of a triangle
_____ / _____

Down

1. a place to keep horses
_____ / _____

2. what is between the beginning and end
_____ / _____

5. the opposite of *big*
_____ / _____

7. the opposite of *aunt*
_____ / _____

Flying Butter

The words have been divided into syllables. Write the missing letter to complete each word. Then, circle the words in the puzzle.

1. ac/____ept

2. big/____est

3. con/____ect

4. co____/tage

5. ra____/bit

6. fu____/nel

7. hob/____y

8. le____/son

9. bu____/ter

10. sum/____er

11. ra____/coon

12. scat/____er

l	w	w	d	r	a	y	h	o	b	b	y
e	c	r	m	a	c	s	p	p	b	i	c
s	y	i	g	c	c	c	z	z	u	g	o
s	y	a	q	c	e	a	k	l	t	g	n
o	n	n	x	o	p	t	f	f	t	e	n
n	f	p	c	o	t	t	a	g	e	s	e
z	m	f	u	n	n	e	l	g	r	t	c
s	u	m	m	e	r	r	a	b	b	i	t

Long Letters

Color the two letters where each word divides into syllables. Then, use the grid to solve the riddle.

	1	2	3	4	5	6	7
14	r	e	p	t	i	l	e
13	u	n	t	i	e		
12	e	n	t	i	r	e	
11	c	o	m	p	e	t	e
10	c	o	m	b	i	n	e
9	i	n	v	i	t	e	
8	d	e	c	i	d	e	
7	l	o	c	a	t	e	
6	e	s	c	a	p	e	
5	m	i	s	u	s	e	
4	m	i	s	t	a	k	e
3	a	d	v	i	c	e	
2	t	e	r	m	i	t	e
1	p	r	e	m	a	d	e

What eight-letter word has only one letter in it?

Answer:

___ ___ ___ ___ ___ ___ ___ ___
(2,14) (2,9) (3,9) (5,11) (6,14) (2,10) (5,6) (2,8)

Bull Without Horns

Read the story. Write the missing part of each compound word. Then, write the compound words on the lines below.

It was a great day for the bullfrog. The sun was shining. The bullfrog went _____side to hop in the forest. Soon, a little red and black _____bug came to the bullfrog. "Good _____noon!" she said.

The bullfrog was hungry. He sat down to have a picnic with the ladybug. Their lunch was some apple_____ and a slice of red _____melon. After lunch, the bullfrog took out a tooth_____ and brushed his teeth.

The bullfrog took off his shoes. He wanted to go _____foot in the river. He walked on the river_____. Soon, a cat_____ jumped from the water. Then, the bullfrog saw a butter_____ in the sky.

Suddenly, the sky turned gray. A drop of water fell on the bullfrog. It was a _____drop. The bullfrog heard a boom. "It is a thunder_____! Time to go home," the bullfrog said.

_____   _____

_____   _____

_____   _____

_____   _____

_____   _____

Basketball Birds

Why did the chicken cross the **basketball** court?

The referee yelled, "Fowl!"

Remove the underlined word part from each word. Then, write a word part from the word bank to make the correct compound word.

back	blue	bull	car	coat	corn	day	down	fall
fish	fly	free	house	pants	rain	side	way	work

1. pop<u>bean</u> _____

2. <u>mud</u>drop _____

3. school<u>hut</u> _____

4. <u>purple</u>bird _____

5. sweat<u>jeans</u> _____

6. door<u>path</u> _____

7. <u>in</u>top _____

8. <u>down</u>yard _____

9. water<u>up</u> _____

10. <u>bike</u>pool _____

11. fire<u>worm</u> _____

12. <u>jelly</u>whale _____

13. <u>cow</u>dog _____

14. care<u>pay</u> _____

15. home<u>play</u> _____

16. <u>night</u>dream _____

17. rain<u>shirt</u> _____

18. <u>turn</u>stairs _____

Cow in an Earthquake

Write at least two compound words that use each word part.

1.   snow

_____
_____
_____

2.   book

_____
_____
_____

3.   berry

_____
_____
_____

4.   some

_____
_____
_____

5.   room

_____
_____
_____

6.   rain

_____
_____
_____

7.   grand

_____
_____
_____

8.   every

_____
_____
_____

Name _____

Dribbling Babies

Each word has the wrong double consonants. Write the words using the correct double consonants.

| ll | pp | rr | ss | tt |

1. clatt _____

2. stiss _____

3. corrar _____

4. leppon _____

5. hally _____

6. cassy _____

7. porrute _____

8. hully _____

9. sossy _____

10. passern _____

11. flisser _____

12. leller _____

Rib-Ticklers Spelling **24**

Tell the Volcano

Unscramble each word. Match each unscrambled word to a letter in the key. To solve the riddle, write the letters in order on the lines below.

Key

full = A   small = U
swell = V   chill = I
miss = A   hiss = O
mass = Y   stiff = L

1. to cool something
   hclil _____chill_____

2. unable to bend
   tifsf _____

3. the opposite of *empty*
   lulf _____

4. to increase in size
   elwls _____

5. to not reach a goal or target
   msis _____

6. how much matter an object has
   sasm _____

7. the sound a snake makes
   sihs _____

8. the opposite of *large*
   sllma _____

What did one volcano **tell** the other volcano?

Answer: __I__ "___ ___ " ___ ___ ___ !

Yellow and Fast

Write the word for each clue. Then, match the symbols under the answers to the symbols below. To solve the riddle, write the correct letters on the lines.

arrange   caterpillar

cattle   dessert

eggplant   million

What is **yellow** and fast?

1. to put items in order

2. a vegetable that is purple

3. the word for this number: 1,000,000

4. an insect that turns into a butterfly

5. something sweet that can be eaten after dinner

6. another word for *cows*

Answer: a banana

  ___   ___   ___ ___ ___ ___ ___

Science Eggs

Use the code to write each word.

Code:	Z	Y	X	W	V	U	T	S	R	Q	P	O	N
Letter:	a	b	c	d	e	f	g	h	i	j	k	l	m

Code:	M	L	K	J	I	H	G	F	E	D	C	B	A
Letter:	n	o	p	q	r	s	t	u	v	w	x	y	z

1. __ __ __ __ __
   X S Z R M

2. __ __ __ __
   X S L K

3. __ __ __ __ __
   H S Z P V

4. __ __ __ __ __
   K R M X S

5. __ __ __ __
   D R H S

6. __ __ __ __ __
   H S V V G

7. __ __ __ __ __
   H S V O O

8. __ __ __ __ __
   G L F X S

27

Elephant Sneeze

Write the correct spelling of each word.

1. lauph

   _____

2. gragh

   _____

3. couph

   _____

4. touff

   _____

5. foto

   _____

6. rouph

   _____

7. enouph

   _____

8. trofy

   _____

9. gogher

   _____

10. alfabet

   _____

Wooden King

Write each word in the correct word box.

| bang | finger | moth | ring | strong | thaw | thorn | thread |

1.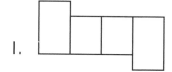

2.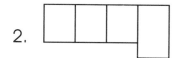

3.

4.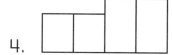

5.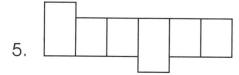

6.

7.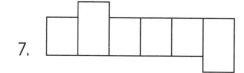

8.

Strawberry Jam

Circle the words in the puzzle. To solve the riddle, write the remaining letters in order on the lines below. Begin at the center of the puzzle.

splash	splint	spray	spread	spring
sprinkle	strike	string	thread	throne

Why was the **strawberry** sad?

Answer:

____ ____ ____ ____ ____ ____ ____ ____ ____ ____ ____!

Name _____

consonant clusters/
digraphs

Springtime Fun

Write the missing letters to complete each word. Then, circle the consonant cluster in each word.

thrill	throat	twelve	twin	twine	scrap
splinter	strap	stripe	string	square	squirt

1. t ____ ____ o ____ t

2. ____ c r ____ p

3. ____ ____ r i p ____

4. s ____ l i n ____ e ____

5. ____ t r ____ n g

6. s q ____ i ____ t

7. s ____ r a ____

8. t ____ r i l ____

9. t w e ____ ____ ____

10. t ____ i n

11. ____ w i n ____

12. s q ____ a r ____

What time of year is it when you are on a trampoline?

Springtime!

© Carson-Dellosa • CD-104387   **31**   Rib-Ticklers Spelling

Team Match

Why don't **matches** play baseball?

One strike and they are out!

UMP

Use the code to write each word.

Code:	Z	Y	X	W	V	U	T	S	R	Q	P	O	N
Letter:	a	b	c	d	e	f	g	h	i	j	k	l	m

Code:	M	L	K	J	I	H	G	F	E	D	C	B	A
Letter:	n	o	p	q	r	s	t	u	v	w	x	y	z

1. ___ ___ ___ ___ ___
  D Z G X S

2. ___ ___ ___ ___ ___
  U V G X S

3. ___ ___ ___ ___
  R G X S

4. ___ ___ ___ ___ ___
  K Z G X S

5. ___ ___ ___ ___ ___ ___
  H G R G X S

6. ___ ___ ___ ___ ___ ___
  X O F G X S

7. ___ ___ ___ ___ ___
  N Z G X S

8. ___ ___ ___ ___ ___
  O Z G X S

9. ___ ___ ___ ___ ___ ___
  H P V G X S

10. ___ ___ ___ ___ ___ ___
  X I F G X S

Misunderstood Storm

Write the missing letter to complete each word. Each word contains the *mis-* prefix. To solve the riddle, write the unused letters from the word bank in order on the lines below.

| a   c   m   e   u   h   m   b   p   l   i   s   n   t   g |

Why did the cloud **misunderstand** the thunderstorm?

1. mi____use

2. misprin____

3. misr____ad

4. mis____ount

5. miss____ell

6. misn____me

7. mis____andle

Answer:

It was ____ ____ ____ ____ ____ ____ ____ ____ !

Dog Tails

Where do dogs go when they need to **replace** their tails?

To **retail** stores!

Circle the l5 words in the puzzle. Each word has the *re-* or *un-* prefix. Then, write the words on the lines.

playunableunlockunwind
unhappyrepayresend
remakerepaintredo
unopununrefturnunt
iefewritteretfillrire

_____ _____ _____

_____ _____ _____

_____ _____ _____

_____ _____ _____

_____ _____ _____

Disappearing One

Unscramble each word. Each word has the *dis-* prefix. Then, write a new word by changing the prefix or the root word.

1. sidliek   _____   _____

2. dsicnonect   _____   _____

3. idscovre   _____   _____

4. sdiagere   _____   _____

5. dsiapprea   _____   _____

6. sidabel   _____   _____

7. iscdard   _____   _____

8. dihsonets   _____   _____

Sleep Cycle

Write each word in the correct word box.

bicycle	bimonthly	biweekly	precut	preheat
premade	preschool	preteen	pretest	preview

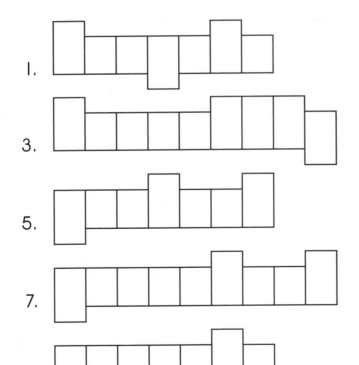

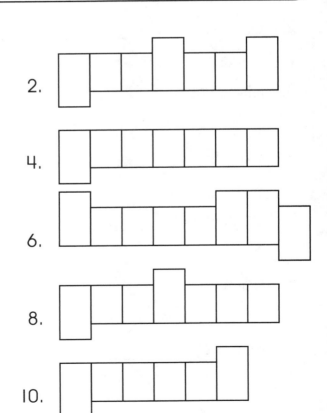

1.
2.
3.
4.
5.
6.
7.
8.
9.
10.

Banana Lotion

Unscramble each word and circle the prefix. Then, complete the crossword puzzle.

Across	**Down**
3. vepriwe _____	1. dsigraee _____
6. repkooc _____	2. kucnol _____
7. etinu _____	4. plerya _____
	5. ccylbie _____

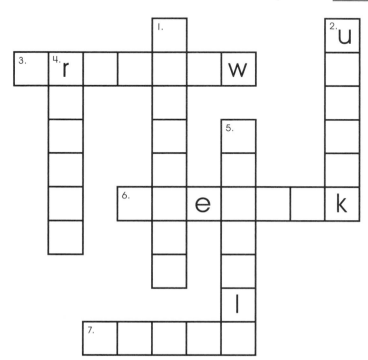

Name _____

Smelly Feet

Add the correct suffix to each word and write it in the correct column.

day   easy   final   friend   happy   loud   lucky

perfect   polite   quiet   real   sad   sudden

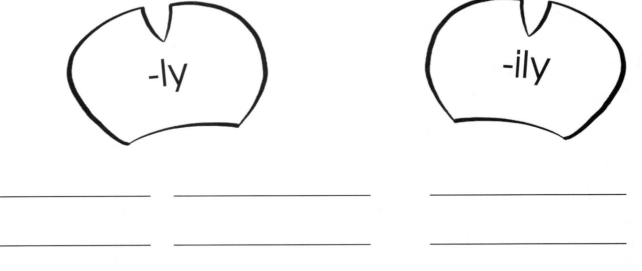

_____   _____   _____

_____   _____   _____

_____   _____   _____

_____   _____   _____

_____

Rib-Ticklers Spelling   **38**   © Carson-Dellosa • CD-104387

The Leopard's Vacation

Find the word in each grid and write it on the line. Each word contains the -*ion* suffix. The letters can connect up, down, left, and right. Start with the underlined letter.

1.

a	t	i
r	e	o
<u>o</u>	p	n

This word means *a surgery to repair a part of the body:*

_____

2.

<u>p</u>	l	u
o	l	t
n	o	i

This word means *man-made waste that harms the environment:* _____

3.

i	t	n
o	n	e
<u>i</u>	n	v

This word means *something that is created by a person's imagination:* _____

4.

a	t	i
c	u	o
<u>e</u>	d	n

This word means *the result of learning in school:*

_____

Name _____

Light in the Darkness

Write the word for each clue. To solve the riddle, write the numbered letters on the correct lines.

> brightness   calmness   coolness   dryness
> emptiness   grumpiness   quietness   shyness

1. a state of being shy around others

2. a state of being quiet

3. a state of being bright

4. a state of being cool

5. a state of being empty

6. a state of being dry

7. a state of being calm

8. a state of being grumpy

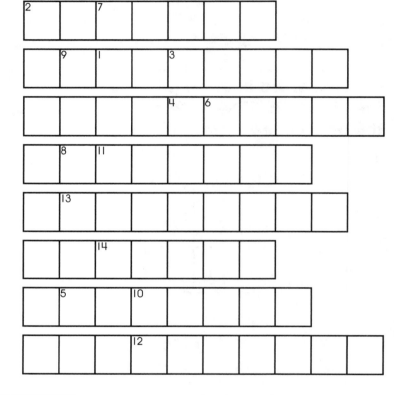

What does a glowworm say when he sees a light in the **darkness**?

Answer:

___ ___ ___ ___ ___ ___
 1   2   3   4   5   6

___ ___ ___ , ___ ___ ___ ___ ___ ?
 7   8   9   10 11 12 13 14

Useless Fisher

Write the opposite of each word. Each opposite word has the -less suffix. To solve the riddle, write the circled letters in order on the lines below.

1. tearful ◯___ ___ ___ ___ ___ ___ ___ ___ ___

2. hopeful ◯___ ___ ___ ___ ___ ___ ___ ___ ___

3. careful ___ ___ ___ ___ ◯___ ___ ___

4. powerful ___ ___ ◯___ ___ ___ ___ ___ ___ ___

5. colorful ◯___ ___ ___ ◯___ ___ ___ ___ ___

6. harmful ___ ___ ◯___ ___ ___ ___

7. painful ___ ___ ___ ___ ___ ___ ◯___

Answer:

She kept eating ___ ___ ___ ___ ___ ___ ___ ___!

Forgetful Monsters

Write your own words to complete each sentence.

1. My pet _____ has such a _____ pair of
                 noun   -ful word

   purple pants.

2. The _____ _____ made a nest on
         -ful word   noun

   a desk.

3. I saw a _____ _____ slide up the
         -ful word   noun

   tree trunk!

4. A tiny _____ skipped on the lily pads in a
           noun

   _____ way.
      -ful word

5. It was _____ to have the huge _____ in
         -ful word   noun

   the garden.

Library Parrot

Circle the 10 words in the puzzle. Each word has a prefix or a suffix. Write the words on the lines.

_____

_____

_____

_____

_____

_____

_____

_____

_____

_____

k	i	n	d	n	e	s	s	y	r
a	w	j	o	y	f	u	l	j	e
t	d	r	v	o	e	j	o	p	s
t	a	l	o	c	a	t	i	o	n
e	r	t	e	a	r	l	e	s	s
n	k	t	w	r	l	i	v	o	y
t	n	z	i	i	e	g	j	p	a
i	e	y	f	h	s	l	n	s	s
o	s	f	w	i	s	h	f	u	l
n	s	w	l	i	g	h	t	l	y
l	o	u	d	l	y	z	l	i	o

43

Detective Carrot

Circle each root word. Then, write a new word using a different root word but the same suffix.

1. k i n d n e s s

_____

2. l o u d l y

_____

3. c a r e l e s s

_____

4. s a d n e s s

_____

5. t e a r f u l

_____

6. r e a l l y

_____

7. a c t i o n

_____

8. w i s h f u l

_____

9. s p o t l e s s

_____

10. d i r e c t i o n

_____

Flavorful Invention

Circle each root word. If a word has a correct suffix, draw a check mark on the line. If a word is spelled with an incorrect suffix, write the word with a correct suffix.

-ful	-less	-ly	-ness	-ion

1. silentness _____

2. quickion _____

3. wingly _____

4. rudeful _____

5. expression _____

6. actful _____

7. tearful _____

8. fitness _____

9. graceness _____

Repeat Who?

Add a correct prefix or suffix to each root word.

bi- dis- mis- pre- re- un-

-ful -ful -ion -less -ly -ness

1. help _____

2. _____ happy

3. _____ view

4. _____ cover

5. power _____

6. _____ cycle

7. _____ spell

8. dark _____

9. color _____

10. act _____

11. _____ pay

12. soft _____

Fearless Robots

Circle each misspelled word. Write the word correctly.

1. Cautness!
Robots on the loose!

_____

2. Bipare for the
race at noon.

_____

3. Displug electronics
to save energy.

_____

4. Please stay motionful
during the
security check.

_____

5. Biturn materials here.

_____

6. How useness is
your robot?

_____

Faster Snail

Write the correct form of each bold word to complete each sentence.

1. The milk is **cheap**.

   The eggs are _____ than the milk.

   The apple is the _____ food in the store.

2. This flower is **short**.

   The grass is _____ than the flower.

   The ants are the _____ things in the garden.

3. Grapes are **sweet**.

   Pineapples are _____ than grapes.

   The peach is the _____ fruit in the bowl.

4. That dress is **nice**.

   These shoes are _____ than the dress.

   This skirt is the _____ piece of clothing.

5. The blanket is **soft**.

   The pillow is _____ than the blanket.

   The mattress is the _____ part of the bed.

6. Her house is **large**.

   Our hotel is _____ than her house.

   That skyscraper is the _____ building in the city.

Sensible Cow

Circle each correctly spelled word and the letter beside it. To solve the riddle, write the circled letters in order on the lines below.

1. acceptible   **a**   acceptable   **h**

2. believible   **n**   believable   **e**

3. questionable   **r**   questionible   **d**

4. edable   **s**   edible   **m**

5. affordable   **o**   affordible   **w**

6. comparable   **o**   comparible   **i**

7. lovible   **n**   lovable   **m**

8. honorible   **s**   honorable   **o**

9. incredible   **o**   incredable   **u**

What did the **sensible** cow pack to wear in Hawaii?

Answer:

_____ _____ _____   " _____ _____ _____ – _____ _____ _____ "

Bugging the Frog

What did the frog say to the fly?

You are really **starting** to bug me!

Add the ending -ing to each word and write it in the correct word box.

boil	burn	complete	create	edit
frame	greet	hike	improve	leap

Drop the *e* and add *ing*

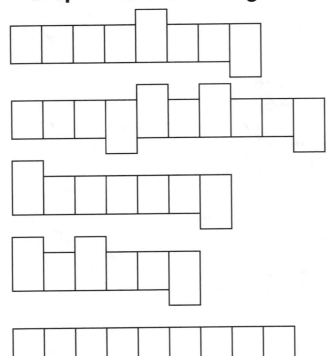

Add *ing*

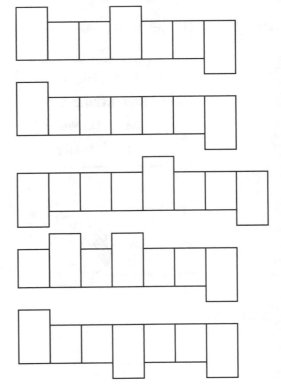

Name _____

Reaching the High Notes

Add the ending -*ing* to each word and write it on the line. Then, circle the words in the puzzle.

1. stop _____
2. drag _____
3. nap _____
4. hop _____
5. shop _____
6. mop _____
7. tag _____
8. clap _____

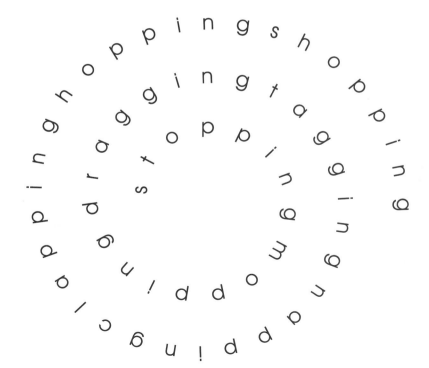

Name _____

Unusual Rabbits

Write the plural form of each word. Then, match the problem numbers to the numbers below. If you added *s*, color the matching spaces red. If you added *es*, color the matching spaces blue. The picture will solve the riddle.

1. bunch _____
2. box _____
3. bench _____
4. match _____
5. hawk _____
6. mask _____
7. dish _____
8. wish _____
9. lamp _____
10. sailor _____
11. fox _____
12. desk _____

What do you call unusual **rabbits?**

Bedtime Animals

Circle each correctly spelled word and the letter beside it. To solve the riddle, write the circled letters in order on the lines below.

1.	knives	y
	knifes	a
	knifis	t

2.	hoofs	u
	hooves	o
	hoovs	h

3.	shelvfs	e
	shelves	u
	shelfs	d

4.	wolves	r
	wolvies	w
	wolfs	p

5.	loafes	w
	loavs	y
	loaves	c

6.	ourselves	a
	ourselfs	l
	ourselvs	c

7.	leavs	o
	leafs	y
	leaves	l

8.	lives	v
	lifs	m
	lifes	t

9.	wifes	s
	wives	e
	wifies	i

10.	halves	s
	halfs	o
	halvs	v

Which animals do you bring to bed?

Answer:

___ ___ ___ ___ ___   ___ ___ ___ ___ ___

Squeaky Mice

Circle each correctly spelled word. Then, write the singular form on the line.

1. childs
   childes
   children
   _____

2. oxen
   oxi
   oxes
   _____

3. basisses
   basi
   bases
   _____

4. tooths
   teeth
   teeths
   _____

5. cacten
   cactuss
   cacti
   _____

6. personi
   people
   persones
   _____

7. potati
   potatos
   potatoes
   _____

8. foots
   feet
   footies
   _____

9. sheeps
   sheep
   sheepes
   _____

10. tomati
    tomatoes
    tomatos
    _____

11. womans
    women
    womens
    _____

12. mice
    mouses
    mices
    _____

"Plane" Paint

Circle each homophone in the story. Then, replace each incorrectly used homophone by writing the correct word above it.

There once was a very plane plain. It had know stripes or colors. It sat buy a fancy plane. The fancy plane was blew and had ate stripes. One night, the plain plane decided to fly. It went up very hi. Too birds zoomed by the plane. The moon shone into the plane's I. It was time to land. The plain plane tried to put on its breaks. But, they were broken! The fancy plane came to help. It through a rope around the plain plane. The plain plane was safe!

Name _____

Dancing Beet

Circle each correctly spelled word and the letter beside it. To solve the riddle, write the circled letters in order on the lines below.

1. woud **N**   wood **I**
2. pail **t**   pahle **u**
3. bee **h**   bie **j**
4. tuo **k**   two **a**
5. bear **d**   bair **s**
6. cent **a**   scennt **l**
7. sew **g**   soo **p**
8. floyur **c**   flower **o**
9. haire **d**   hare **o**
10. knight **d**   niht **b**
11. heel **b**   heul **y**
12. meat **e**   meete **w**
13. paire **u**   pear **a**
14. foir **h**   four **t**

Why did the beet dance to the music?

Answer: ____ ____ ____ ____ ____ ____

____ ____ ____ ____ ____ ____ ____ ____ !

Name _____

Knight's Bedtime

Complete the crossword puzzle. Match the symbols in the puzzle to the symbols below. To solve the riddle, write the correct letters on the lines.

knee   knife   knight   knock   know   knowledge

Down

1. a tool with a sharp edge that is used to cut things
3. Let's _____ on the door to see if someone is home.
4. I _____ what you are talking about.

Across

2. a man who wore armor and kept a kingdom safe during the Middle Ages
3. a part of the body that allows the leg to bend
5. information

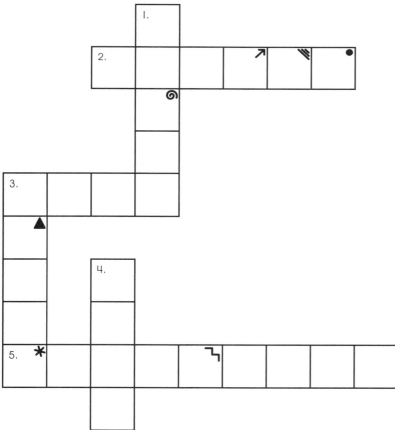

What does a young **knight** need in his bedroom?

Answer:

a "___ ___ ___ ___ ___ ___ ___ — ___ ___ ___ ___ ___"
　 ✳ ▲ ⊚ ↗ ⧷ • 　 ⌐ ⊚ ↗ ⧷ •

© Carson-Dellosa • CD-104387   **57**   Rib-Ticklers Spelling

Wrinkly Grape

Write the word for each clue on each row of grapes. Match the symbols in the answers to the symbols below. To solve the riddle, write the correct letters on the lines.

| unwrap | wrap | wreck | wrench | wrist | write | wrong |

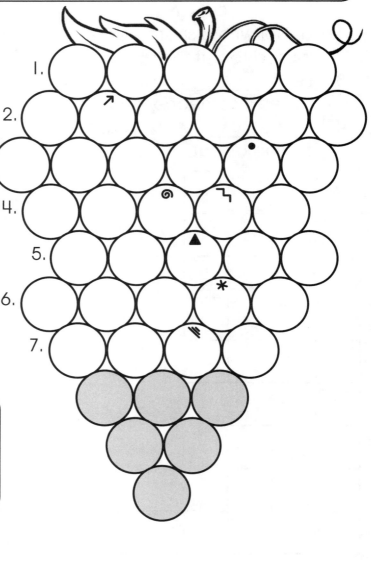

1. a ship that sank in the ocean
2. a tool that turns nuts and bolts
3. to take off the outside of a gift
4. the part of your arm that connects to your hand
5. to put words onto paper with a pen or pencil
6. another word for *incorrect*
7. to put paper on a gift

What do you call a **wrinkly** grape?

Answer:

___ ___ ___ ___ ___ ___ ___
⬘   ↗   •   ◉   ⅂   ▲   *

Whale Band

What do you call a whale band?

Write the word for each clue. To solve the riddle, write the circled letters in order on the lines below.

| castle | comb | doubt | heir | hour | lamb | listen | often |

1. a word that means *frequently* ◯ ___ ___ ___ ___

2. a person who inherits money or property ___ ___ ◯

3. what untangles your hair ◯ ___ ___ ___

4. a baby sheep ___ ◯ ___ ___

5. to try to hear something ___ ___ ◯ ___ ___

6. what you have when you are not sure about something ___ ___ ___ ___ ◯

7. it has 60 minutes ___ ___ ◯ ___

8. a large building where a king and queen may live ___ ◯ ___ ___ ___ ___

Answer:

an " ___ ___ ___ – ___ ___ ___ ___ "

Quiet Lambs

Help the shepherdess gather her sheep. Draw a line through each word that has a silent letter.

START

castle

sled

curl

romp

wrap

gnat

troop

snug

climb

knock

thumb

clump

fly

plant

would

comb

FINISH

Taffy Train

What do you call a train loaded with taffy?

Draw an X on each misspelled word. To solve the riddle, write the remaining bold letters in order from left to right and top to bottom on the lines below.

minimum **a**	vacume **i**	hieght **t**	lightning **c**	embarrass **h**
absense **r**	separate **e**	recieve **n**	neighbor **w**	disapear **s**
believe **c**	librery **p**	accomplish **h**	parallel **e**	wierd **l**
guarantee **w**	fourty **o**	business **t**	official **r**	useage **k**
independant **h**	piece **a**	straiht **j**	succeed **i**	although **n**

Answer:

_____ " _____ _____ _____ — _____ _____ _____ _____ _____ "

_____ _____ _____ _____ _____

Rib-Ticklers Spelling

Vegetable Vacation

Where did the vegetables stay during their vacation?

Write the word for each clue. To solve the riddle, write the letters from the bold boxes in order on the lines below.

| brilliant | calendar | courage | government |
| license | misspell | persuade | |

1. a permit to drive a car

2. the ability to do something brave

3. the organization that rules a nation

4. very smart

5. to get someone to do something

6. a chart that shows the days, weeks, and months of a year

7. to spell a word incorrectly

Answer:

The "____ ____ ____ ____ ____ ____ ____" Inn

Lizard Laughs

Draw a line through each word to complete the maze. Letters can connect up, down, left, and right. The first word has been done for you.

achieve
twelfth
familiar
particular
appropriate
surprise
accessible
knowledge
sincerely
maintenance

START

a	c	b	h	e	s	u	s	e
x	h	f	t	t	l	r	i	a
e	i	l	h	a	i	p	r	c
v	s	e	f	i	r	s	e	c
e	t	w	a	x	p	s	e	c
u	p	i	m	a	o	i	c	e
a	i	l	w	p	r	b	l	c
r	m	c	u	p	g	v	e	n
p	v	i	l	a	o	n	k	a
a	r	t	a	r	w	m	a	n
s	e	g	d	e	l	y	i	e
i	n	c	e	r	e	l	n	t

FINISH

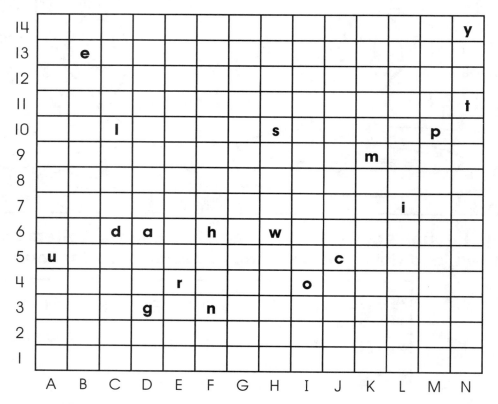
Coordinate Spelling

Use the grid to write each word.

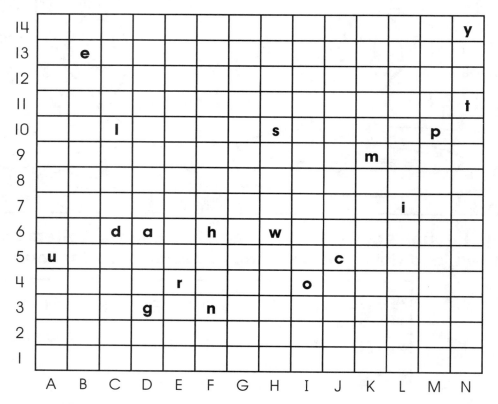

1. ____ ____ ____ ____ ____ ____ ____
   (H,10) (M,10) (B,13) (J,5) (L,7) (D,6) (C,10)

2. ____ ____ ____ ____ ____
   (M,10) (L,7) (B,13) (J,5) (B,13)

3. ____ ____ ____ ____ ____ ____ ____ ____
   (H,10) (J,5) (F,6) (B,13) (C,6) (A,5) (C,10) (B,13)

4. ____ ____ ____ ____ ____ ____ ____ ____
   (N,11) (I,4) (K,9) (I,4) (E,4) (E,4) (I,4) (H,6)

5. ____ ____ ____ ____ ____ ____ ____ ____ ____
   (F,3) (B,13) (J,5) (B,13) (H,10) (H,10) (D,6) (E,4) (N,14)

6. ____ ____ ____ ____ ____
   (H,6) (B,13) (L,7) (E,4) (C,6)

Name _____  commonly misspelled words

Lightning in the Lab

Circle the extra letter in each word. To solve the riddle, write the circled letters in order on the lines below.

Why was there thunder and lightning in the lab?

1. recommbend
2. privrilege
3. immaediately
4. surpriise
5. familniar
6. dissappear
7. accomplitsh
8. sinceorely
9. congraturlations
10. minimmum
11. hieight
12. extraorndinary
13. restgaurant

Answer: The scientists were

__ __ __ __ __ __ __ __ __ __ __ __ __ !

© Carson-Dellosa • CD-104387   **65**   Rib-Ticklers Spelling

Where Fish Don't Go

Circle two words in each book title that make a contraction. Then, write the contraction on the line.

1. *The Day I Could Not Swim* by I. M. Sunk _____

2. *Shrimp Secrets You Do Not Want to Know* by R. U. Stinky _____

3. *Sharks Have Not Been Here* by P. H. Yoo _____

4. *Your School Is Not as Cool as My School* by Gold E. Fish _____

5. *I Will Not Be on a Pizza* by Ann Chovy _____

6. *Shore Chores Are Not Fun!* by K. P. Cool _____

7. *They Were Not Worms!* by I. M. Hooked _____

8. *Sally Has Not Seen the Sky* by Stu Dent _____

9   *I Would Not Like Being a Frog* by Tad Pole _____

10. *It Had Not Sunk In* by I. M. Shipwrecked _____

11. *The Octopus Should Not Buy Gloves* by Tommy Hands _____

12. *The Jellyfish Does Not Like Peanut Butter* by R. U. Hungry _____

Frog Car

Write a contraction using the word in parentheses and *have* to complete each sentence.

1. If (you) _____ ever been swimming before, raise your hand.

2. I think that (they) _____ gone to the zoo.

3. Maggie (would) _____ called us if she wanted to go to the park.

4. The flowers (we) _____ picked smell so good!

5. Anton (might) _____ eaten lunch already.

6. The teacher thinks that (I) _____ made the best painting in the class!

7. Carmon (could) _____ told me that there was no school today!

8. I think that Omar (should) _____ done his homework before class.

© Carson-Dellosa • CD-104387 **67** Rib-Ticklers Spelling

Name _____

I'm a Crumby Cookie

Circle the pair of words in each cookie that can make a contraction. Then, write the contraction on the line.

1.

2.

3.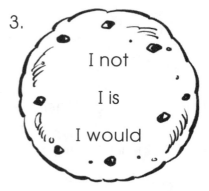

_____   _____   _____

4.

5.

6.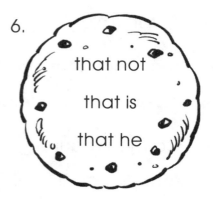

_____   _____   _____

Friendly Beaver

Circle the nine pairs of words in the puzzle that can make contractions. Then, write the contractions on the lines.

Cowboy Boots

What did the boots say to the cowboy?

You ride; I'll go on foot.

Circle each misspelled contraction in the story. Write the correct spelling of each contraction on the line.

Rodeo Riley is a tough cowboy. He'l win any contest he's in. "Whatl'l he do next?" everyone asked. The prize at the next contest was a pair of cowboy boots. "I bet they'ill be comfortable!" Rodeo Riley said. He'd been in a lot of contests. "This'l be the best one," he told his friend Opal. She's a cowgirl who is the fastest rider in town. "Let's be a team in the contest," Opal said. "We'ull beat everyone in the lasso competition!" At the contest, there were many people watching. "Wh'oll win?" they asked. Rodeo Riley and Opal went into the ring. "Th'eyll lasso that barrel in five seconds," said someone in the crowd. "Tha'tll be impossible," another rider told the person. But, Rodeo Riley and Opal did win the contest! They each got a brand-new pair of shiny black cowboy boots.

_____   _____

_____   _____

_____   _____

_____   _____

Grumpy Turtle

Why's the turtle so grumpy?

Draw an X on each misspelled word. To solve the riddle, write the remaining bold letters in order from left to right and top to bottom on the lines below.

the'yd	she'd	you'd	Im'	he'd	your'e
t	**s**	**n**	**h**	**a**	**i**
you're	w'ed	hed'	they'd	Id'	yo'ure
p	**d**	**e**	**p**	**r**	**s**
sh'ed	I'm	yo'ud	we'd	h'ed	I'd
j	**i**	**h**	**n**	**e**	**g**

Answer:

He's a ____ ____ ____ ____ ____ ____ ____ ____ ____ turtle!

Fanciest Animal

What's the fanciest animal in the world?

A diamondback rattlesnake!

Write the contraction for each pair of words. Then, complete the crossword puzzle.

Across

5. we + have _____

6. you + will _____

7. I + will _____

9. who + have _____

10. it + is _____

Down

1. who + will _____

2. they + are _____

3. I + had _____

4. could + have _____

5. will + not _____

8. could + not _____

10. I + am _____

No Haircut!

Circle the contraction that completes each sentence.

1. Do you think _____ good at jumping rope?

   A. he'd   B. she's   C. we've   D. let's

2. _____ it time to go to lunch?

   A. Can't   B. There've   C. Isn't   D. It'd

3. I _____ be able to play after school today.

   A. won't   B. can't   C. we'd   D. weren't

4. Gabriel _____ know where we are going to meet him.

   A. would've   B. we're   C. he's   D. doesn't

5. You _____ allowed to stay out late.

   A. isn't   B. aren't   C. here's   D. won't

6. _____ be on vacation all week.

   A. There'd   B. They'll   C. They've   D. Don't

7. I didn't know that _____ on the soccer team.

   A. you'd   B. you're   C. you've   D. you'll

8. She _____ see very well without her glasses.

   A. can't   B. wasn't   C. aren't   D. would've

Name _____

What's the Scoop?

Write the contraction for each pair of words.

1. should have
2. there have
3. were not
4. they would
5. here is
6. is not
7. who is
8. let us
9. it would
10. he would
11. I am

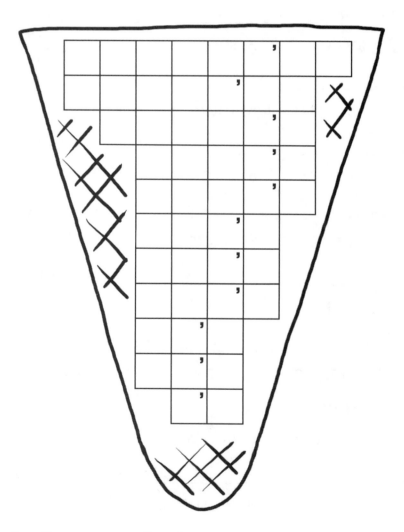

Page 5
1. bang; 2. pale; 3. tale; 4. cane; 5. yam;
6. catch; 7. same; 8. bait; 9. task; alley cats

Page 6

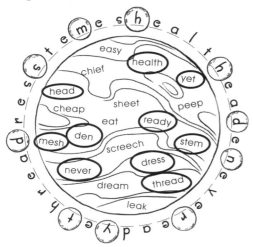

Page 7
1. sick; 2. wick; 3. hike; 4. sigh; 5. slip; 6. fiber;
7. title; 8. dice; 9. style; 10. wire; a dandelion

Page 8
1. toast; 2. fox; 3. going; 4. rope; 5. bone;
6. quote; 7. loaf; 8. chop; 9. lock; 10. joke;
11. rock; a "fire-quacker"

Page 9
words in yellow boxes: cube, mute, cute,
huge, fuel, use, rescue, few, unit, bugle,
music, value, menu, pupil, usual, argue, view,
beauty, review, human; words in red boxes:
much, fuzz, tusk, puff, rush, plus, drum, buzz,
dunk, bump, hush, dusk, hut, lump, nut

Page 10
1. eight; 2. people; 3. straight; 4. steak;
5. receive; 6. height; 7. island; 8. though;
9. beauty; 10. sew; 11. buy; It "over-swept"!

Page 11

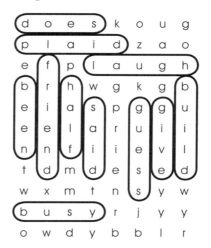

Page 12
short oo: cook, good, hood, stood,
wood, woof

long oo: bloom, boom, mood, stool,
tool, zoom

Page 13
1. fern; 2. burn; 3. turn; 4. verb; 5. bird; 6. dirt;
7. chirp; 8. nurse; 9. germ; He pulled on its ears!

Page 14

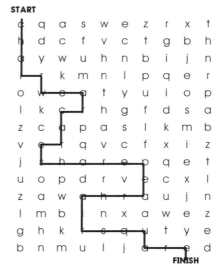

Page 15

	Word	Syllables	First syllable		Second syllable	
1.	quickly	quick/ly	5	(N)	2	M
2.	comfort	com/fort	3	a	4	(e)
3.	plastic	plas/tic	4	(i)	3	l
4.	surface	sur/face	3	s	4	(t)
5.	display	dis/play	3	o	4	(h)
6.	witness	wit/ness	3	f	4	(e)
7.	problem	prob/lem	4	(r)	3	s
8.	vulture	vul/ture	3	u	4	(s)
9.	kingdom	king/dom	4	(i)	3	e
10.	thunder	thun/der	4	(d)	3	b
11.	jacket	jack/et	4	(e)	2	n
12.	lobster	lob/ster	3	c	4	(w)
13.	program	pro/gram	3	j	4	(i)
14.	capture	cap/ture	3	p	4	(n)
15.	forward	for/ward	3	(i)	4	(s)
16.	trumpet	trum/pet	4	(l)	3	Y
17.	chapter	chap/ter	4	(t)	3	k
18.	tortoise	tor/toise	3	h	5	(s)
19.	blanket	blan/ket	4	(a)	3	a
20.	crystal	crys/tal	4	(t)	3	l
21.	fancy	fan/cy	3	(n)	2	b
22.	construct	con/struct	3	d	6	(e)

Neither side wins. It's a tie.

Page 16

1, 3, 6, 9, 12, and 14 should be circled; 2. re/duce; 4. fi/nal; 5. ho/tel; 7. si/lent; 8. la/bel; 10. ba/by; 11. ro/bot; 13. mo/ment; a river

Page 17

The underlined letters in each word should be circled. 1. crea/ture; 2. cau/tion; 3. au/thor; 4. ex/plain; 5. jour/ney; 6. fea/ture; 7. sweat/er; 8. mois/ture; 9. pay/ment; 10. foun/tain; 11. re/ceive; 12. wea/sel; 13. trou/ble; 14. moun/tain; 15. mead/ow

Page 18

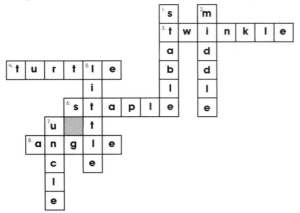

Across: 3. twin/kle; 4. tur/tle; 6. sta/ple; 8. an/gle; Down: 1. sta/ble; 2. mid/dle; 5. lit/tle; 7. un/cle

Page 19

1. ac/cept; 2. big/gest; 3. con/nect; 4. cot/tage; 5. rab/bit; 6. fun/nel; 7. hob/by; 8. les/son; 9. but/ter; 10. sum/mer; 11. rac/coon; 12. scat/ter

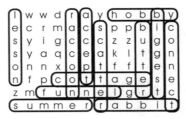

Page 20

	1	2	3	4	5	6	7
14	r	e	p	t	i	l	e
13	u	n	t	i	e		
12	e	n	t	i	r	e	
11	c	o	m	p	e	t	e
10	c	o	m	b	i	n	e
9	i	n	v	i	t	e	
8	d	e	c	i	d	e	
7	l	o	c	a	t	e	
6	e	s	c	a	p	e	
5	m	i	s	u	s	e	
4	m	i	s	t	a	k	e
3	a	d	v	i	c	e	
2	t	e	r	m	i	t	e
1	p	r	e	m	a	d	e

envelope

Page 21

From left to right and top to bottom: outside, ladybug, afternoon, applesauce, watermelon, toothbrush, barefoot, riverbank (riverbed), catfish, butterfly, raindrop, thunderstorm (thunderclap)

Page 22

1. popcorn; 2. raindrop; 3. schoolhouse; 4. bluebird; 5. sweatpants; 6. doorway; 7. inside; 8. backyard; 9. waterfall; 10. carpool; 11. firefly; 12. jellyfish; 13. bulldog; 14. carefree; 15. homework; 16. daydream; 17. raincoat; 18. downstairs

Page 23

Answers will vary.

Page 24

1. class; 2. still; 3. collar; 4. lesson; 5. happy; 6. carry; 7. pollute; 8. hurry; 9. sorry; 10. pattern; 11. flipper (flitter); 12. letter (lesser)

Answer Key

Page 25
1. chill; 2. stiff; 3. full; 4. swell; 5. miss;
6. mass; 7. hiss; 8. small; I "lava" you!

Page 26
1. arrange; 2. eggplant; 3. million;
4. caterpillar; 5 dessert; 6. cattle;
a banana in a race car

Page 27
1. chain; 2. chop; 3. shake; 4. pinch;
5. wish; 6. sheet; 7. shell; 8. touch

Page 28
1. laugh; 2. graph; 3. cough; 4. tough;
5. photo; 6. rough; 7. enough; 8. trophy;
9. gopher; 10. alphabet

Page 29
1. bang; 2. ring; 3. thaw; 4. moth; 5. finger;
6. thorn; 7. strong; 8. thread

Page 30

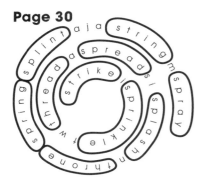

It was in a jam!

Page 31
1. throat, thr; 2. scrap, scr; 3. stripe, str;
4. splinter, spl; 5. string, str; 6. squirt, squ;
7. strap, str; 8. thrill, thr; 9. twelve, tw;
10. twin, tw; 11. twine, tw; 12. square, squ

Page 32
1. watch; 2. fetch; 3. itch; 4. patch; 5. stitch;
6. clutch; 7. match; 8. latch; 9. sketch;
10. crutch

Page 33
1. misuse; 2. misprint; 3. misread;
4. miscount; 5. misspell; 6. misname;
7. mishandle; It was mumbling!

Page 34

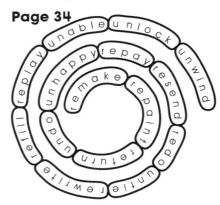

Page 35
1. dislike; 2. disconnect; 3. discover;
4. disagree; 5. disappear; 6. disable;
7. discard; 8. dishonest; New words will vary.

Page 36
1. bicycle; 2. pretest (preheat); 3. bimonthly;
4. preview; 5. preheat (pretest); 6. biweekly;
7. preschool; 8. preteen; 9. premade;
10. precut

Page 37

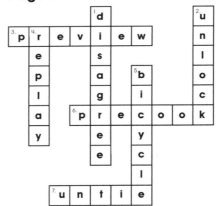

Page 38
-ly words: suddenly, really, quietly, finally,
perfectly, politely, friendly, loudly, sadly;
-ily words: luckily, happily, easily, daily

© Carson-Dellosa • CD-104387 **77** Rib-Ticklers Spelling

Page 39

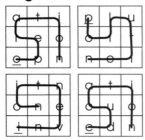

1. operation; 2. pollution; 3. invention;
4. education

Page 40

1. shyness; 2. quietness; 3. brightness;
4. coolness; 5. emptiness; 5. dryness;
7. calmness; 8. grumpiness; Is that you,
Mommy?

Page 41

1. tearless; 2. hopeless; 3. careless;
4. powerless; 5. colorless; 6. harmless;
7. painless; She kept eating the worms!

Page 42

Answers will vary.

Page 43

k	i	n	d	n	e	s	s	y	r
a	w	j	o	y	f	u	l	j	e
t	d	r	v	o	e	w	o	p	s
t	a	l	o	c	a	t	i	o	n
e	r	t	e	a	r	l	e	s	s
n	k	t	w	r	l	i	d	o	y
t	n	z	i	i	e	g	j	p	a
i	e	y	f	h	s	l	n	s	s
o	s	f	w	i	s	h	f	u	l
n	s	w	l	i	g	h	t	l	y
l	o	u	d	l	y	z	l	i	o

Page 44

Root words: 1. kind; 2. loud; 3. care; 4. sad;
5. tear; 6. real; 7. act; 8. wish; 9. spot;
10. direct; New words will vary.

Page 45

Root words: 1. silent; 2. quick; 3. wing; 4. rude;
5. express; 6. act; 7. tear; 8. fit; 9. grace; Words
should be corrected as follows: 2. quickly
(quickness); 3. wingless; 4. rudeness (rudely);
6. action; 9. graceful (graceless)

Page 46

1. helpful or helpless; 2. unhappy; 3. review or
preview; 4. discover, uncover, or recover;
5. powerful or powerless; 6. bicycle or recycle;
7. misspell or respell; 8. darkness or darkly;
9. colorless or colorful; 10. action; 11. repay or
prepay; 12. softly or softness

Page 47

1. Caution; 2. Prepare; 3. Unplug;
4. motionless; 5. Return; 6. useful

Page 48

1. cheaper, cheapest; 2. shorter, shortest;
3. sweeter, sweetest; 4. nicer, nicest;
5. softer, softest; 6. larger, largest

Page 49

1. acceptable; 2. believable; 3. questionable;
4. edible; 5. affordable; 6. comparable;
7. lovable; 8. honorable; 9. incredible;
her "moo-moo"

Page 50

drop the *e* words: creating, completing,
framing, hiking, improving;
add *ing* words: boiling, burning, greeting,
editing, leaping

Page 51

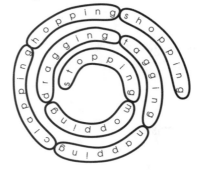

Answer Key

Page 52

-es words: 1. bunches; 2. boxes; 3. benches; 4. matches; 7. dishes; 8. wishes; 11. foxes;

-s words: 5. hawks; 6. masks; 9. lamps; 10. sailors; 12. desks

Page 53

1. knives; 2. hooves; 3. shelves; 4. wolves; 5. loaves; 6. ourselves; 7. leaves; 8. lives; 9. wives; 10. halves; your calves

Page 54

1. children, child; 2. oxen, ox; 3. bases, base; 4. teeth, tooth; 5. cacti, cactus; 6. people, person; 7. potatoes, potato; 8. feet, foot; 9. sheep, sheep; 10. tomatoes, tomato; 11. women, woman; 12. mice, mouse

Page 55

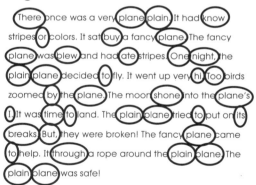

Answers from left to right and top to bottom: Their, plain, plane, no, by, blue, eight, high, Two, eye, brakes, threw

Page 56

1. wood; 2. pail; 3. bee; 4. two; 5. bear; 6. cent; 7. sew; 8. flower; 9. hare; 10. knight; 11. heel; 12. meat; 13. pear; 14. four; It had a good beat!

Page 57

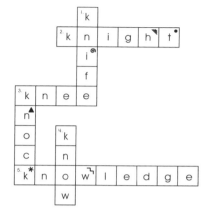

a "knight-light"

Page 58

1. wreck; 2. wrench; 3. unwrap; 4. wrist; 5. write; 6. wrong; 7. wrap; a raisin

Page 59

1. often; 2. heir; 3. comb; 4. lamb; 5. listen; 6. doubt; 7. hour; 8. castle; an "orca-stra"

Page 60

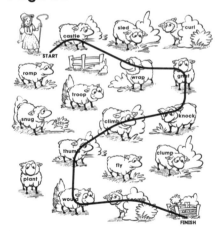

Page 61

Correctly spelled words in order from left to right: minimum, lightning, embarrass, separate, neighbor, believe, accomplish, parallel, guarantee, business, official, piece, succeed, although; a "chew-chew" train

Page 62

1. license; 2. courage; 3. government; 4. brilliant; 5. persuade; 6. calendar; 7. misspell; The "Lettuce" Inn

Page 63

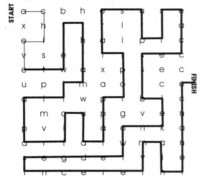

Page 64

1. special; 2. piece; 3. schedule;
4. tomorrow; 5. necessary; 6. weird

Page 65

The extra letters are: 1. b; 2. r; 3. a; 4. i; 5. n;
6. s; 7. t; 8. o; 9. r; 10. m; 11. i; 12. n; 13. g; The
scientists were brainstorming!

Page 66

1. Couldn't; 2. Don't; 3. Haven't; 4. Isn't;
5. Won't; 6. Aren't; 7. Weren't; 8. Hasn't;
9. Wouldn't; 10. Hadn't; 11. Shouldn't;
12. Doesn't

Page 67

1. you've; 2. they've; 3. would've;
4. we've; 5. might've; 6. I've;
7. could've; 8. should've

Page 68

1. you're; 2. we're; 3. I'd; 4. they're; 5. let's;
6. that's

Page 69

Page 69 (continued)

it's, she's, he's, what's, there's, it's, that's,
who's, here's

Page 70

Correctly spelled contractions in order: He'll,
What'll, they'll, This'll, We'll, Who'll, They'll,
That'll

Page 71

Correctly spelled contractions in order from
left to right: she'd, you'd, he'd, you're, they'd,
I'm, we'd, I'd; He's a snapping turtle!

Page 72

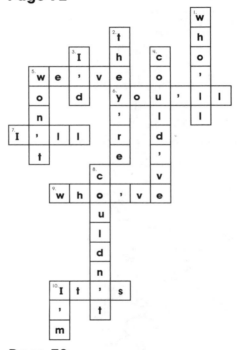

Page 73

1. B; 2. C; 3. A; 4. D; 5. B; 6. B; 7. B; 8. A

Page 74

1. should've; 2. there've; 3. weren't; 4. they'd;
5. here's; 6. isn't; 7. who's; 8. let's; 9. it'd;
10. he'd; 11. I'm